Stephen Walsh

HIGH BALL TO THE WEE MAN

Scotland's World Cup years in poems -
each, like the best Scottish dances,
being in strict tempo

First published in Great Britain in 2025

by CHapbooks, Horsham, West Sussex RH13 0LE

ISBN 978-1-9162521-2-7

Contents

1 1974 page 5

FOUR SONNETS FOR BIG JOE AND WEE BILLY

2 1978 page 11

THREE VILLANELLES FOR ARCHIE GEMMILL

3 1982 page 17

JUST THE ONE GHAZAL FOR MILLER AND HANSEN

4 1986 page 21

EIGHT INTERLOCKING RUBAIYAT FOR WEE DIEGO

5 1990 page 33

SIX CANTOS IN OTTAVA RIMA FOR MOMOSUPERMOSUPERMAURICEJOHNSTON

6 1998 page 59

EDDIE GRAY'S ELEGY

Born and brought up in Edinburgh and then Glasgow, Stephen Walsh left Scotland to go to university and has never quite managed to get back home. Married, with five grown up children, he is a knackered old teacher most of the time but has found time to write three prose books and three poetry collections. Like James Joyce in exile nostalgically reciting the names of all the shops in O'Connell Street, he spends his Saturday afternoons listening to Open All Mikes on Radio Scotland.

For Helena, of whom it can be said

(like many Scottish football heroes of the past):

'though she be but little she is fierce'

1974

Four Sonnets for Big Joe & Wee Billy

Poems are like football formations, best described in numbers. With their 14 lines in iambic pentameter, sonnets are an old fashioned 4-4-(4)-2, tactically-speaking. Like Johan Cruyff, however, they have a turn, so they can usefully encapsulate those familiar football moments when sweetness turns to bitterness, and the odd occasion when it works the other way round.

West Germany, 1974

World Cup Qualifying

26 September 1973, 8 pm

Scotland	**2**	**Czechoslovakia**	**1**
Holton 41, Jordan 72		Nehoda 33	
Hampden Park, Glasgow			95,786

World Cup Group 2

14 June 1974, 7.30 pm

Zaire	**0**	**Scotland**	**2**
		Lorimer 26, Jordan 34	
Westfalenstadion, Dortmund			25,800

18 June 1974, 7.30 pm

Scotland	**0**	**Brazil**	**0**
Waldstadion, Frankfurt			62,000

22 June 1974, 4.00 pm

Scotland	**1**	**Yugoslavia**	**1**
Jordan 88		Karasi 81	
Waldstadion, Frankfurt			56,000

Group 2 Table	W	D	L	F	A	Pts
Yugoslavia (Q)	1	2	0	10	1	4
Brazil (Q)	1	2	0	3	0	4
Scotland	1	2	0	3	1	4
Zaire	0	0	3	0	14	0

Scotland did not qualify for the second stage.

I

Czechoslovakia

I had the golden ticket from a boy at school.
        From up the Celtic End the Czechs, in white,
Looked like Subbuteo men, but in the throaty night,
        Fags sparking round the noise-and-smoky bowl,
This was a big boys' game. See when the Six-Foot-Two-
        Eyes-of-Blue Big Jim came up from the back,
Climbed high and beat the goalie in the Yashin black,
        My floodlit eyes exploded into blue.

When Billy hit the post, I lost my friend. The sway -
        I'd been on tiptoes - carried me away
Like Peter Pan. We thought we'd scored. Right then, we did -
        As Willie's cross met Big Joe's toothless heid
The crowd surged forward, wild, again, and I was then
        A lost boy hugged by strangers. Full grown men.

2

Zaire

Early next day Grandad went down to Dobbie's Loan -
    Not for his half and a half, for a TV.
Radio Rentals, eight pounds down, the luxury -
    Our first World Cup in colour. I'd leave home
On match days - yellow bus or blue train - then I'd go
    Across the green and up the common stair.
You could say, for the Zaire game, that 'I was there' -
    Just not in Dortmund. Up Dumbarton Road.

What an atmosphere, but. We were expecting goals.
    We'd tartan girls on cans, and sausage rolls.
On screen, a red pipe band burst out a giant ball,
    Like their defender who burst out the wall
And booted the ball out. We laughed. *The stupit clown!*
    Scotland scored two. Then, stupid, closed it down.

3

Brazil

We all recall how that hot night panned out. No score,
        But Scotland so on top. What might have been.
All over them. The Tartan Army of the Rhine
        All singing *We'll Support You Evermore*.
Sure, that Brazilian team was more Brazil in name
        Than nature. There are colours that run.
Not fit to wear the shirt. Pelé, Tostão, Gerson gone.
        The roles reversed - they kicked *us* out the game.

But still, it hurts. We're in the second half. Big Joe
        Heads it. Their goalie, Felix, fluffs - it goes
To Bremner, two yards out, just slightly to one side,
        And he pokes out a toe; the ball squirms wide.
'My granny's granny could have scored that,' Grandad said.
        It's our *pietà*: Billy, holding his head.

4

Yugoslavia

So - home, without being beat. A special Scotland trick.
        I wasn't home, for I'd ducked out to see
A girl I knew, after the match. The ABC.
        'Aff winching,' Grandad laughed. *Earthquake*. The flicks.
Another bright blue night. A different sort of heat.
        Joe's goal too little and too late, so now
It was a different game of how far can you go -
        A big boy's game. After, on Renfield Street,

We're waiting on the bus. A man stomps by, deaf-blind
        To his family, twenty yards behind.
The head-scarfed wifey scowls, watching him disappear,
        Their little lost boy bringing up the rear
Wanting his hug from dad. He cries. He asks his mum,
        'What's wrang wi' da?' She sighs. 'His team lost, son.'

1978

Three Villanelles for Archie Gemmill

The villanelle is a Wembley Wizard of a poetic form, creating dazzling patterns all over the blank page of the pitch. The first and third lines pop up again and again at strategic points, like a pair of old-fashioned wingers, and turn up again in the final seconds to kill the game off. For all its trickery it can create a familiar feeling – that of a repeated experience the reader is fated to relive time and time again.

Argentina, 1978

World Cup Group 4

3 June 1978, 4.45 pm

Scotland	**1**	**Peru**	**3**
Jordan 14		Cueto 43, Cubillas 71,77	
Estadio Chateau Carreras, Córdoba			37,927

16 June 1998, 4.30 pm

Iran	**1**	**Scotland**	**1**
Eskandarian (og) 43		Danayfar 60	
Estadio Chateau Carreras, Córdoba			7,938

11 June 1978, 4.45 pm

Scotland	**3**	**Netherlands**	**2**
Dalglish 44, Gemmill 46, 68		Rensenbrink 33, Rep 71	
Estadio Ciudad de Mendoza			35,130

Group 4 Table	W	D	L	F	A	Pts
Peru (Q)	2	1	0	7	2	5
Netherlands (Q)	1	1	1	5	3	3
Scotland	1	1	1	5	6	3
Iran	0	1	2	2	8	1

Scotland did not qualify for the second stage.

I

'Enter through one of the old turnstiles, and watch Archie Gemmill score one of the World Cup goals of all time' ***(Scottish Football Museum brochure)***

I'm watching that goal Archie Gemmill scored
On a museum loop at Hampden, on TV.
It makes it three-one - Scotland need one more -

But what a game. The Dutch score early doors
And shut up shop; we've got a back door key.
One-each, two-one, then little Archie scores,

And *oh, oh, oh, it's magic* - the furores
(Beat by Peru, held by Iran, Wee
Bud sent home, for drugs) vamoose. One more!

On the telly you can hear the ragtag corps
Of Ally's Army raise a sunstroked plea,
For - after Archie dribbles through and scores -

We've twenty minutes, still, to get the four.
Don't cry for us, Argentina! For we
Will walk a million miles for just one more…

Shooting in the dark, of course. The roar
Dies down and we go home. But I still see
How Archie weaves his magic way, then scores -
This loop in which we'll always need one more.

2

'I haven't felt that good since Archie Gemmill scored against Holland in 1978...'
(Irvine Welsh/ John Hodge, *Trainspotting*)

I watched that Holland game on the TV
In a public bar on the Kilmarnock Road.
This auld yin, Prostate Tam, went for a pee

To beat the half time rush, and King Kenny
Chose that moment to meet Big Joe's offload -
Re-enter Tam, effing at the TV.

We weren't eighteen, but no one checked ID
In World Cup year. 'Olé, Ola!' we roared,
At the team, and at Tam, who'd nipped out for a pee

And came back to find he'd missed the penalty,
Though Archie hadn't. Hearing him explode,
We peed ourselves - and, later, on TV,

When Archie slalomed through to make it three
You know where Tam had gone. Joy overflowed -
He ran in with his knob still out, pee

Dribbling down his legs, and, bladdered, he
Raised his arms, like Archie when he scored.
And no-one thought how short-lived things can be
As Scotland made it three-one on TV.

3

'Archie Gemmill kindly asked the Dutch to dance to the tune of a lone piper...'
(Eduardo Galeano, *Football in Sun and Shadow*)

That bar burned down, but now they've manikins
At this museum where you can *be* Archie.
You dribble, beat three 'men' and knock it in -

It's magic. You forget your kids, the din,
The other Archie's voice on the TV.
The Dutch are statuesque – they're manikins,

In ghost-white, not orange, uncoloured-in,
As if the past *is* another country
For whom they, faded, play. So get tore in.

Somewhere in the background someone sings
'I Have A Dream'. A piped crowd chants 'Easy!'
You wouldn't bet against the manikins

Playing some of the Scotland teams you've seen,
But you can seize the day and make it three.
First make your dummy run and chip it in,

Then cock one arm. The shadow of a grin
Will mirror all your guts and (vain)glory.
You beat three men – well, maybe manikins -
Then, like Archie, you knocked the football in.

1982

Just The One Ghazal For Miller and Hansen

A ghazal is a series of couplets, each ending with a combination of a rhyming word and a repeated phrase. Such tightness sounds like a suffocating catenaccio or (for younger readers) a high press, but the effect is often fluid. The ghazal is by tradition a melancholy expression of loss, disappointment or the fading of youthful love. Any resemblance to the experience of watching football is no doubt accidental.

Spain, 1982

World Cup Group F

15 June 1982, 9.00 pm			
Scotland	**5**	**New Zealand**	**2**
Dalglish 18, Wark 29, 32		Sumner 54, Woodin 64	
Robertson 73, Archibald 79			
La Rosaleda, Málaga			36,000

18 June 1982, 9.00 pm			
Brazil	**4**	**Scotland**	**1**
Zico 33, Oscar 49, Eder 65		Narey 18	
Falcao 87			
Estadio Benito Villamarín, Seville			47,379

21 June 1982, 9.00 pm			
USSR	**2**	**Scotland**	**2**
Chivadze 60, Shengelia 85		Jordan 15, Souness 87	
La Rosaleda, Málaga			45,000

Group 4 Table	W	D	L	F	A	Pts
Brazil (Q)	3	0	0	10	2	**6**
USSR (Q)	1	1	1	6	4	**3**
Scotland	1	1	1	8	8	**3**
New Zealand	0	0	3	2	12	**0**

Scotland did not qualify for the second stage.

1

We call those 1970s World Cups a hard luck story -
A Look-At-Brave-Wee-Scotland-Showing-Guts-And-Pluck story.

'74's a classic case. Unbeaten, in our first World Cup
For yonks. Yabbadabbadoo! But it's an Awe-Struck story,

For we could and should. Two more against Zaire, we'd have been through! -
But first game, safety first. A Should-Have-Run-Amuck story.

And how could we know Brazil weren't good that year? The wee man doffs
His cap to the giants of the game. That Star-Struck story-

line prefaced the final act when, the ball being on the slates,
We played the doomed-heroic-Scotland-Never-Chuck-It story.

2

The same but different in '78. High hopes brought low.
Peru, Iran. A proper How-We-Came-Unstuck story,

With added hubris, too. The song ('Ally's Army'). The massed bands
At the Hampden send-off. A full-on Hit-By-A-Truck story,

Outrage stoked by tabloid tales of money squabbles in the camp
(Tomorrow's chips love a good Where-There's-Brass-There's-Muck story).

Yet we've always had Mendoza, and Archie's pyrrhic goal,
The old Redemption-From-The-Jaws-Of-Fate-Was-Plucked story.

3

So, '82. The song's 'I Have A Dream'. We're in ironic
Mode, affecting a Look-Let's-Face-It-We-Just-Suck story.

That Cup's typecasting central. Brazilians stroll. Italians scream.
Germans score penalties. Our bit part's a Lame Duck story

Of self-inflicted wounds. Against New Zealand we're determined
To skip the First-Match-Failed-To-Shoot-The-Sitting-Duck story,

But at three-nil McGrain gifts them a goal with a crap back pass,
And though it finishes 5-2 to us the Nae Luck story's

Seeds are sown. Against Brazil (a great Brazil this time) we wake
The Titans' wrath. Their hammers ring a Thunder-Struck story,

And Alan Rough stands petrified as heaven's fire rains down,
With an open-mouthed cartoon face from a Donald Duck story.

4

It's Russia in the last match. We have to win. We score. We Have
A Dream again. They equalise. It's a Nip-And-Tuck story,

Till Miller and Hansen do that 'After-You-Claude'-hopping act,
A sort of 'Chuckle-Brothers?-Meet-Your-Uncle-Buck' story,

Bumping into each other like pub team centre-backs, letting
The Russian through, and out we go. The Record-Got-Stuck story's

Back in the groove. Back home early again. A hard luck story?
Naw. By now we knew the Scotland-World-Cup-Clusterfuck story.

1986

Eight Interlocking Rubaiyat for Wee Diego

Arabs and Scots share a love of sherbet, though in Glasgow they call it a wee sherbet. The most famous examples of rubaiyat, an Arabic quatrain, were written by the wine-addicted Omar Khayyam, whose work is filled with the conflicted and melancholic feelings of love and pain familiar to all those who have ingested Buckfast, or any of the other 'refreshments' Scotland fans traditionally favour, on a Football Special.

Mexico, 1986

Friendly Match
2 June 1979, 3.00 pm

Scotland	**1**	**Argentina**	**3**
Graham 85		Luque 33 60, Maradona 70	
Hampden Park, Glasgow			61,918

World Cup Group E
4 June 1986, 11.00 pm

Scotland	**0**	**Denmark**	**1**
		Elkjaer 58	
Estadio Universidad de Neza			18,000

8 June 1986, 7.00 pm

Scotland	**1**	**West Germany**	**2**
Strachan 18		Voller 22, Allofs 50	
Estadio Corregidora, Querétaro			30,000

13 June 1986, 7.00 pm

Uruguay	**0**	**Scotland**	**0**
Estadio Universidad de Neza			36,000

Group E Table	W	D	L	F	A	Pts
Denmark (Q)	3	0	0	6	3	**6**
W. Germany (Q)	1	1	1	3	4	**3**
Uruguay (Q)	0	2	1	2	7	**2**
Scotland	0	1	2	1	3	**1**

Scotland did not qualify for the second stage.

Quarter Final
22 June 1986, 7 pm

England	**1**	**Argentina**	**2**
Lineker 81		Maradona 51, 55	
Azteca Stadium, Mexico City			114,580

England did not qualify for the semi-finals.

'Remembrance of things past is not necessarily the remembrance of things as they were.' **(Marcel Proust, *A La Recherche de Temps Perdu*)**

I

You'll know about Proust and his madeleines -
How smells could take him back to childhood scenes.
The same for me. A bag of chips, I'm there
At Scotland games at Hampden in my teens.

We were the business in brushed denim flares
And purple nylon shirts. Our blow-dried hair
Sat proud. It wafted with a Vosene gleam.
Our shoes platformed us in the smoky air.

Standing Room Only, for almost any team,
On terraced slopes 'where there ran golden streams,'
(A Big Yin gag) 'and wild beasts wandered free.'
Macaroon bars, spearmint gum: our field of dreams,

And we were there, our team - Hugh, Chas, Danny -
For Finland, Spain, the Swiss, both Germanies.
The Czechs, not once but twice. We'd see it live,
Then hotfoot home for highlights on TV,

Though on the way, of course, on the Queen's Drive
Or Viccy Road, we'd stop for chips. A hive
Of steamy breath as we relived the scenes.
On freezing nights our dead hands would revive.

We'd Danny's flag (the motto would have been
'REMEMBER BANNOCKBURN, 1314')
And if you'd been there those nights then you'd have seen
Us standing there booing 'God Save The Queen'.

2

That crew turned motley. First, our shoes shrank down.
Danny permed his hair – loose-curl, tight-wound.
Chas took to camel coats; Hugh was his twin.
I'd desert boots and hair like Jackson Browne.

I guess that we were changing, boys to men,
But some things never changed. In Spring, back then,
We'd play England, Northern Ireland and Wales.
Same time next year, we'd play them all again,

Though England was the big one. Heads v. Tails.
Black v White. Auld Enmity. The World Cup paled
Alongside the big match of the year:
Red Barrel versus Tartan Special Ales.

I only got to watch it on TV,
But Danny, with his flag, went to Wembley,
Got on the pitch, and from that human zoo
Brought back a chunk of turf which he showed me

As proof we'd turned their patch of green to blue.
Yet here at home no flower of Scotland grew.
At every match, the tune was still royal.
At every match we'd stand only to boo.

By now there was an edge to our recoil
With devolution coming to the boil -
A political nudge to be (dis)loyal.
I'd stickers on my schoolbooks: SCOTLAND'S OIL.

3

One morning I woke up with great big feet.
While I was wearing flares they'd felt petite,
But *che sera, sera*. What will, will be.
It was '79. Those flares were obsolete.

Danny left school and went to Germany
To be a waiter. He wanted to 'live free'.
He made a toffee sign, pushed his nose up,
Whenever I said 'university',

While Chas and Hugh went in their father's pub.
One straight-legged game before we all broke up -
Argentina, to see this new star play,
Some seventeen-year-old they had. Some pup.

Diego won his first cap that hot day.
The game was men and boys, round the wrong way -
For that Boy Wonder, floating like a ghost,
Supermanned us - up, up, and away,

With stops, starts, flicks, back-heels. A feint, a boast.
Like it's a game with kids, he sprints, then coasts.
The Scotland goalie comes, and then backs off
To No-Man's-Land. He scores, at the near post.

A long goodbye before we all took off,
With further hints the monarch could eff off.
But - *noblesse oblige* - at him we didn't scoff.
The crowd at Hampden clapped that young king off.

4

By 1985 I was exiled -
An English wife, and soon an English child.
English teaching, too. Cords, Lennon specs,
A cardy, brogues. That whole young fogey style.

Soon getting north for games became complex.
Not just Scotland, Hibs too. I'd 'life-projects' -
AKA excuses not to go
To crap grounds, and crapper football. The effect?

Hampden missed me. So did Easter Road.
Hearts led the league. That was a further blow -
That season they were playing like Madrid.
Through that winter they had a proper go,

A bona-fide full-fat title bid
Which went to the last day, then hit the skids
Away at Dens. The Hearts were two points clear.
Dundee brought on a sub called Albert Kidd,

And he scored two. It's sad, but true - I cheered.
Sadder, but true – I still mock 'jambo tears'.
Uber-schadenfreude. Tribal glee.
Kidd was made Hibs' Player of the Year.

It's *infra dig*, childish, such enmity -
You know you should grow up, yet love to see
Your nearest (not your dearest) on their knees.
Poor Hearts were that. My Auldest Enemy.

5

Now '86 was sad (we'd lost Jock Stein).
The year of those wee signs ('John 3:16').
Not much else comes to mind. That World Cup was
A case of never was, not might have been.

Our blue kit had a white belt. Further flaws
Were clear in a strange play-off game in Oz.
We edged them here, flew over to their side
And fluked the nil-nillest of nil-nil draws.

We then found out the formbook hadn't lied -
Drawn in the Group of Death, we duly died.
Two losses (Denmark, Germany). A draw
(Nil-nil, again) with Uruguay, a side

Whose ten men scratched and kicked us off the ball
As we screamed *animuls*. In all that fall
Just one iconic moment glistered, shone -
Wee Strachan, with his foot up on the wall

When we led Germany. Small man syndrome.
I watched in England, home away from home,
With English friends whose joy watered my fears -
For England were making Mexico their own.

We needed a Messiah - one appeared.
He'd aged and put on weight - cocaine and beer.
Boy king no longer - still without a peer.
Diego - Scotland's Player of the Year.

6

John Milton, scratching blindly with his pen
Said he'd 'Justify The Ways Of God To Men'.
My theme, too, is Divine Providence -
To Justify the *Hand* of God to them.

The scene is the Azteca. Bright. Intense.
The fiery heat of a battle that commenced
On Goose Green and Bluff Cove four years ago.
That handball is redemption. Recompense.

We'd no high horse. Back in the day, Big Joe
Did it to Wales. We didn't want to know.
It's not cheating until it's done to you.
The Hand of Jaws, the Hand of Diego.

But when the Young Pretender slaloms through
Mad Dogs and Englishmen to make it two,
He scatters all thoughts of morality.
A cheat? Maybe. But a Wembley Wizard too -

Every inch a king, a new Archie.
While we've not yet invented 'ABE'
A deep-set feeling in these Scottish bones
Has a phrase for it. *Get It Right Up Yi…*

Fair play to him! In those Englishmen's homes
I tsk-tsk, sympathise and guard my tone.
Inside's a gratitude I don't make known -
To Diego. 'Wee man'. One of our own.

7

Back to my teenage years. We Scotland fans,
Sardined on the old terraces and stands,
Would sing in gleeful unison: 'If you...
If you hate the effing English, clap your hands.'

I clapped. And old-man-slippered now, ask who
I thought it was that I was singing to?
My lovely wife's English, my dear late
Dad. My effing kids are effing English too.

Easy, back then, to mouth that strong word 'hate'.
We had it pat. Glencoe. The crofters' fate.
Cheviot, Stag and Oil. Cumberland's force.
Our strong word for their strong power to dictate.

Grandad mouthed *his* tale, of troops of horse,
Tanks in George Square. Milder for me, of course.
Just a backwash, a swill of history
(The Falklands, Poll Tax, Brexit) from one source.

But surely things have changed. Time has changed me,
And Scotland too. At Hampden now you'll see
Us sing our song, with no chorus of boos.
We got our ticket for the game, Maggie,

So it's surely time to edge towards a truce.
For it is only a game. Or an excuse.
People I love. Sorry for being obtuse.
I don't hate you. I just want you to lose.

8

Ach well. *Tempus fugit.* Age and youth.
We live and learn. We grow. We find our truth.
So many reasons these days not to say
That we hate Jimmy Hill 'cause… it's uncouth.

I thought of Danny just the other day -
Saw a photo of a perm, recalled the way
He'd bring his dad's old Playboys into school
And flash the tits and beaver of Miss May

On the school bus. At thirteen, that was cool.
At sixteen, though? You know youth can be cruel -
Like her, he'd faded. We were buying fags,
The NME, and he'd become a fool.

Though football kept us tight, the reddest rag
To our big bull was that he wore that flag -
Sometimes shouldered, sometimes flying free -
To games. It was embarrassing. We nagged,

Then we had words. He said it was lucky.
We peed ourselves. 'Lucky? Scotland?' But he
Dug in his heels, and wouldn't be seen dead.
So we dumped him, the camel coats and me,

When, down the Hampden stairs one night, he led
Through the stramash. 'Follow the flag,' he said.
We watched it go, then went the other way,
Laughing like drains. But pleasure will be paid,

For, half an hour's slow walk later, when we
Were lined up in the dark outside Guidi's,
There was Danny, blue flag uneclipsed,
Bright, Hopperesque, inside. 'So what kept yis?'

He waved us up the queue in fellowship,
Quite unaware we'd given him the slip -
And we followed our flag home, our fingertips
Warming in the scent of salty chips.

1990

Six Cantos in Ottava Rima for MoMoSuperMoSuperMauriceJohnston

Ottava Rima may sound like part of a no-nonsense Italian centre-half partnership of another era, but it takes a cavalier, free-flowing approach to the poetry game reminiscent of the great Brazilian side of 1970. Like that team (Pelé was a terrible man for the women, while Gerson had a man whose job it was to light his half-time cigarettes) the form has a louche side. Lord Byron used it for 'Don Juan', thinking it an apt vehicle for his descriptions of the low-grade antics of a philandering hero.

Italy, 1990

World Cup Group C

11 June 1990, 4.00 pm			
Scotland	**0**	**Costa Rica**	**1**
		Cayasso 48	
Stadio Luigi Ferraris, Genoa			30,867

16 June 1990, 8.00 pm			
Sweden	**1**	**Scotland**	**2**
Stromberg 86		McCall 11, Johnston 81	
Stadio Luigi Ferraris, Genoa			31,283

20 June 1990, 8.00 pm			
Scotland	**0**	**Brazil**	**1**
		Muller 82	
Stadio delle Alpi, Torino			62,502

Group C Table	W	D	L	F	A	Pts
Brazil (Q)	3	0	0	4	1	**6**
Costa Rica (Q)	2	0	1	3	2	**4**
Scotland	1	0	2	2	3	**2**
Sweden	0	0	3	3	6	**0**

Scotland did not qualify for the second stage.

'We're going to deep-fry your pizza, deep-fry your pizza...'
(Tartan Army chant at Italia '90)

I

Father Time is like a full-back, overlapping.
Four years fly by and, Christ, I'm no spring chicken -
A toddler's at my feet; a newborn's napping,
Mattressed on a midriff midlife's thickened.
But though Age comes tiki-taka tippy-tapping,
World Cups remind you you're alive. And kicking...
    Ciao, Italia '90! *Nessun' Dorma*[1]!
    Four weeks you can forget Death's round the corner.

Now growing old's no fun. The body weakens.
The prostate starts to swell. The eyes go watery.
You can feel just like the Last of the Mohicans
When you recall all your youthful bampottery -
Stuff you did that doesn't get a peek in
As you go grey and deaf and dumb and doddery.
    Well, there's some echo of this midlife crisis
    In our latest squad's rank failure to entice us,

For sad to say the times have been a-changing.
The giants of our game - our gods, wing-footed -
Have aged and given way, and this guard-changing
Has seen the puny for the mighty substituted.
Ormond and Stein are dead; Fergie's arranging
A life elsewhere; so Minions sit, shell-suited,
    Where Once Were Kings. From up here in the cheap seats
    We don't need specs to see our team is dugmeat.

---

[1] 'Nessun Dorma', as sung by Luciano Pavarotti, was the theme for the BBC World Cup coverage in 1990. It is an aria from Puccini's opera *Turandot*, the plot of which resembles a World Cup group; the hero, Prince Calaf, must surmount three challenges or endure eternal shame. Not to be confused with 'Just One Cornetto'.

The manager, for one. Jeez, how he loves a platitude
('A team is like a choir, and you can tune it'.)
He talks like some new Jesus, whose beatitude
Is 'Blessed Are the Men who Make a Unit'[2].
He comes to change our hearts and minds and attitudes.
Combed hair. Clean face. A bit of a balloon. It
        Would need you to be thinking pretty loosely
        To confuse Signor Roxburgh for *Il Duce*[3].

Look at the team photie. No Mac's excluded -
McLeish, MacLeod, McStay, McCall, McKimmie -
But tbh, it's fairy-dust-denuded.
Good Scots as proud as any See-You-Jimmy,
But as Alan Hansen[4] might well have concluded
You'll not win anything with patronymy.
        Our heroes of the past had household names.
        These aren't household names in their ain hames.

---

[2] In the interests of strict accuracy, I ought to say that Andy Roxburgh, the Scotland 'manager' from 1986-1993, didn't actually say any of these things. He did however come over as a bit of a balloon, especially to those of us brought up on the hard men that predated him, such as Willie Ormond, Alex Ferguson and Jock Stein, all mentioned here. The fact that he had been a primary school teacher in his other life may not have helped his credibility. The main signal of his modernising tendency was his insistence on his job being rebranded. He was called 'national coach' and not, like his illustrious forebears, team manager.

[3] At least he made the trains run on time. Mussolini, that is, not Andy Roxburgh.

[4] Alan Hansen played suavely for Partick Thistle, Liverpool and Scotland and pundited, equally suavely, for the BBC. He is uncharitably remembered elsewhere in these poems for his contribution to our exit from the World Cup of 1982. I'm sure he never expressed any opinion one way or another about playing a load of players whose name began with Mac. However, on an episode of 'Match of the Day' in 1995, having watched Manchester United lose their opening match of the season, he expressed the view that 'you will never win anything with 'kids'. The kids in question were David Beckham, Paul Scholes and the Neville Brothers, and they went on to win the championship.

'The Mighty Fallen.' I might fall - to fury.
They aren't all Macs - if I could even care less -
But Bett, Fleck and Levein don't reassure me,
And as one who saw Jordan, Dalglish and Souness[5]
I'm hardly mollified by 'Juke Box' Durie.
As Frazer in 'Dad's Army'[6] says, *We're Doooomed.* Best
        Let Hope sleep, like this baby on my belly -
        Or mute it, like the volume on the telly.

These guys aren't charlatans. They aren't transgressors.
They don't deserve grilling on my rotisserie.
But match them with their manly predecessors -
They're mere boys who lack the mystique and the mystery
Of the Wembley Wizards or the Scotch Professors.
We sing about our history, but history
        Moves on, hearts do grow o-o-old. Oh, brother -
        It's just one fucking thing after another.

---

[5] 'Big Joe' Jordan and 'King Kenny' Dalglish need no introduction, and I only footnote Graeme Souness as an excuse to include Archie Gemmill's description of him: 'If he was made of chocolate he would eat himself'. The other players named all had decent careers, in spite of being tarnished by not being as good as their forerunners. Craig 'Mr Magoo' Levein went on the manage Scotland from 2009-12. His regnal period is best remembered for his sending out a team to play the Czech Republic in Prague in an 4-6-0 formation. In spite of parking the bus across several spaces, Scotland still contrived to lose.

[6] The sitcom 'Dad's Army' ran on the BBC from 1968-1977. The characters are members of a Home Guard regiment guarding a fictional town called Warmington-on-Sea during World War Two. They are a ramshackle bunch of flatfooted bank managers, woollen-scarved mummy's boys and moustachioed shysters. Several of the characters are in the Home Guard because they are too old for active service - these include Private Frazer, played by the gaunt-faced John Laurie. He is the local undertaker who, having been brought up in the Isle of Barra, has a well-developed sense of Calvinistic pessimism. Hence this catchphrase, which usually comes at the end of one of his setpiece catastrophizing anecdotes.

'Ignore the past and you're doomed to repeat it.'
Oh, what I wouldn't give... the past was banterous.
So easy now to slink away, defeated.
But it's a World Cup! You can't hide, cantankerous...
That cathode glow you see is where I'm seated -
A Braveheart of the Sofa, Tam O'Shanterous.
    As true fans know (for all the fear that fills you)
    It's the hope, not the despair, that's going to kill you.
    There's not much we can do to slow Time's footfall -
    But we can make sure we dinnae miss the football.

2

The Scotsman's headline (Dateline: Costa Rica)
Is WARNING, THEY'RE BEATABLE. It feels hubristic.
For though I know it's to be taken tongue in cheek, a
Chill fills me when we wax optimistic.
I know we have a dream, but can't we seek a
Line less super and a bit more fragilistic?
        There's loose-tongued talk of butchers and of bakers,
        Of their plucky part-time candlestick makers.

The late great BBC man David Francey[7]
Was commentating live once, on the air. He
Saw a Chilean do something fancy,
And asked his name (he was working in a pair). The
Summariser muttered something chancy,
The 'gist' being that he didn't know or care. We
        Heard David speak the name on radio
        Just as he'd *heard* it said: 'Fuctivano'.

---

[7] David Francey (1924-2011) was the voice of Radio Scotland's football coverage during the golden years and through a good few dross ones as well. His catchphrases were legion – 'a drive', 'it's all over', and 'oh dear, oh dear,' the last of which is (ever so subtly) slipped in to this passage. The apocryphal nature of the famous 'Fuctivano' story is evident from the many different teams that Fuctivano has come to play for over the years, while the taciturn summariser has been identified variously as the gruff Rangers captain John Greig and the erudite Glasgow Herald journalist Ian Archer. Thrillingly, I met David Francey once, when he was voicing a radio series I was involved in. I sat on his hotel room bed drinking his whisky – he was away from home for a couple of days and had decided, in a low-key Presbyterian sort of way, to make a night of it – and after a couple of drinks I dared to ask him about Fuctivano. He conspicuously declined to say that the story was untrue. I had the impression he thought it was quite funny, though he may have been being polite (he was a lovely man). Either way he didn't, as I had hoped, say, 'Oh dear, oh dear.'

Oh dear, oh dear! David! Stand in the corner!
Though your mistake - a lack of common sense
When mugging up the gen on Johnny Foreigner -
Is a long-held Scotland flaw. Due diligence?
We seem to hire inferior informers,
And lack (more ways than one) intelligence.
We're hardly MI5, but it's a blunder
To give our spying jobs to Stevie Wonder.

We've history in this, and it's a bummer.
In '54, the coach, one Andy Beattie,
Took our team to Switzerland at height of Summer
In hobnail boots and shirts equally meaty.
Our officials, Mr Dumb and Mr Dumber,
Were blind and deaf to all Beattie's entreaties.
We clumped and sweated, got hung out to dry, and
Lost seven-nil to the silk-clad Uruguayans[8].

[8] Tommy Docherty, who managed Scotland in the early 1970s before taking over at Manchester United, was in the 1954 squad, and (especially in after-dinner-speech mode in his twilight years) was vocal in criticising this fiasco-ridden campaign. He described how Beattie 'quit as soon as our plane touched down' following a row with the officials, and was replaced by the trainer. Scotland took only 13 players ('to make room for the officials' wives') and the team was equipped in what he called 'prison shirts'. He went on: 'Imagine playing in a Crombie overcoat. Our shorts went past our knees, the socks were double-knit and of course we had big, clumpy Mansfield Hotspurs on our feet. The Uruguayans' boots were sleek and they wore ultra-thin vests. In the boiling heat we were knackered before the end of their anthem which, typically of South American countries, went on forever.'

Then there was my nightmare, Argentina.
We were drawn to play the 'veteran' Peruvians.
Our sleuths said we would take them to the cleaners
As they were 'past their best', 'antediluvian'.
But, come the day, they frisked like inbetweeners.
With his free kicks, so youthfully Vesuvian,
        Cubillas[9] showed our 'gen' was blazered bluffing.
        We don't call them the SFA for nothing.

This time their hot tip's that the Ticos' goalie
Is a wee man. Our Andy doesn't dally.
He picks a team with wingers telt to wholly
Pelt high balls, as if the game's Aunt Sally,
Towards a front line tall, thin and beanpole-y.
The Light Brigade's charge into their Death Valley
        Ended up being less of a blind alley
        Than pumping high balls to Alan McInally[10].

---

[9] Teofilo Cubillas was the undoubted star of the Peru team of 1978, and of many Subbuteo teams of the period. (Peru was a popular team to own in the 1970s, as their strip had a red diagonal flash, which was almost impossibly exotic; I still have mine in the attic.) The real-life Peru's role in the 1978 World Cup, however, is widely regarded as suspect. Having played well to beat Scotland and draw with the eventual finalists Netherlands in the first group stage, they then faced an Argentina team who needed to win by four clear goals to go through. A variety of conspiracy theories has emerged over the years to explain the 6-0 win for the eventual winners.

[10] The Costa Rica goalie, as it turned out, was not a wee man at all. Luis Gabelo Conejo was 6' 2 tall and was later chosen by FIFA as one of the players of the tournament. The 'plucky part timers' who were representing Costa Rica had actually won the CONCACAF championship in 1989, ahead of the USA. Maurice Malpas of Dundee United, who was a significant member of the 1990 squad, later said: 'Looking back now, Costa Rica were a decent side. They were technically very gifted. I don't think we underestimated them. It was just a case that we didn't really know too much about them.'

The part-timers from across the wide Sargasso
Are soon swaggering like it's their side that's got Fate on.
Marchena does a midfield dance, a *paso*,
Leaves Malpas for dead and turns the pace on.
Jara backheels smartly to Cayasso,
Who bops it through the bandy legs of Leighton.
        The forty minutes left amount to nothing,
        For all our Big Bad Wolf huffing and puffing.

The Tartan Army's booing says how painful
It is to watch your team lose as you swelter.
Discarded tartan scarves make acid rainfall
As our bashed team, abashed, legs it for shelter.
Spaniards twirl white hankies when disdainful,
But our tradition's different - we give pelters.
        The old joke: any team can have a bad day,
        But how come ours is always on a Sat'day?
        At home, the headlines change. There'll be no let-off.
        STOP THE WORLD, they say. WE WANT TO GET OFF[11].

---

[11] STOP THE WORLD, WE WANT TO GET OFF was the Daily Record's headline on the day after the Costa Rica match. This was just part of a contumelious reaction to the defeat, with the Evening Times' Alan Davidson writing grandiloquently that Scotland had 'joined the ranks of the great unwashed of world football.' It offers an interesting insight into the world-view of Scottish football writers (aka 'fans with typewriters') of the period. There were some serious delusions of grandeur amongst the Scottish soccerati of the time.

3

Now 'Coach' Roxburgh's a kind of Captain Sensible.
His persona is the clean-living newcomer.
Urbane, well spoken, calm, focussed, forensical,
He says that Scotland's habits don't become her,
And that our love of 'flawed genius' is nonsensical[12].
He thinks a swally never made a summer,
        And wants his team to live a life of purity
        As tedious as my own mid-life maturity.

Do you remember this saga historical?
How Jimmy Johnstone's team-mates, whisky-addled,
Put him to sea in an unseaworthy coracle[13] -
Jinky was rescued, oarless and bedraggled,
By the coastguard. How's that for metaphorical?
Scotland - up Shit Creek, without a paddle.
        A squad of drunken sailors, playful, frisky,
        With educated feet - and tastes for whisky.

---

[12] Some of these were actually world- class players, like Hughie Gallacher (the Wembley Wizard whose decline began when he started having his post-match pints before the game) and Denis Law (who, along with Joe Baker, wrote off a nearly-new Alfa Romeo Giulietta during his short stay with Torino). Intermediate bampots include Jimmy Johnstone (as described), Willie Johnston (sent home from Argentina in 1978, and sent off 21 times in his career) and Frank McAvennie ('whose tipple was nipple'). Finally there is a cast of thousands rarely heard of outside their native land, including golden legend-in-their-own lunchtime names like Vic Kasule, Chic Charnley and Andy Ritchie. There are many amusing/ alarming (delete as applicable) stories about these in Stuart Cosgrove's wonderful book *Hampden Babylon.*

[13] The Scotland squad were in their training camp at Largs for the week of the 1974 Home Internationals when this incident occurred, much as described. When a sheepish Johnstone came down to breakfast the next day, he was greeted by shouts of 'Come in Number 7, your time is up' and a rousing chorus of 'Michael Row the Boat Ashore'. 'Jinky' laughed that off but was not so happy with the press reports which appeared in the subsequent days. Consequently he offered a 'salute' (as described later) to the gentlemen of the press in their eyrie high above the old Hampden stands, after the stirring victory over England.

You always sensed that sense of contradiction
In the best years that I saw Scotland play.
We liked to win, of course, but loathed restriction,
And played the game (of life!) quixotic-ly.
Jinky's team, for all its dereliction,
Thumped England the subsequent Saturday.
    As Wee Jinky, shirtless, V-signed the press box, we
    Carolled our national unorthodoxy.

Re: drunken stars, I could get anecdotal.[14]
Jim Baxter[15], now, was capably deep-thrappled.
In the lounge bar of the old Saint Enoch Hotel,
Slim Jim, tempted, ate of the boozy apple.
He could make Georgie Best look teetotal,
And took Puskas to a hoorhouse in Drumchapel!
    You might live in a mansion or a poor house -
    You wouldny want him round for tea at your house.

---

14 Sadly, there was no room in this canto, for all my attempts to squeeze it into pentameter, for the famous song of Scotland players of this era: 'We drink beer, we drink wine/ We're the Scotland forward line.'

15 Jim Baxter had a princely liking for Italian suits and operated out of the lounge bar of the St Enoch Hotel, in the city centre, where he dined on smoked salmon sandwiches washed down with vintage champagne and did not always pay his bill. He would often come for training at Ibrox smelling of booze; John Greig recalled the 'times when (Baxter) came into training so drunk that he couldn't bite his fingers and he would just go through and lie in the bath trying to recover.' He sometimes did his warmups reading the 'Racing Post'. Many Scots of his generation felt he was 'the greatest', though he could be his own worst enemy. He liked, in his phrase to 'extract the urine' when his team was on top; an Austrian player who took unkindly to this broke his leg in Vienna. He left Rangers after a dispute about money and his brilliant promise faded at Sunderland and Nottingham Forest before he returned to Ibrox as a bloated shadow of his former self. Inevitably, and foolishly, he ran pubs in his dotage and his relationship with the profits was nothing if not predictable. He died, in his early sixties, of liver-related problems.

But at Wembley, with his socks around his ankles,
And Alan Ball in chase like some wee puppy,
He sits down on the ball. This riles and rankles
Ramsey's men, but that's not all, for up he
Shakes and shimmies, leaving them in tangles,
And, uber-gallus, starts playing keepy-uppy.
    He ran them ragged, made them all look silly -
    Turned World Cup Winners into World Cup Willies.[16]

Now I've said our squad's the bland leading the blander,
Made up of whatshisname and whodyacallit.
But there's a wildcard pick, one rough outlander
Whose name slides like an oyster off the palate.
Like those heroes of old he's a philanderer -
A Jack the Lad, as subtle as a mallet.
    We didn't break the mould! A spotty Herbert
    Who likes a bet, the birds, the fags, a sherbet.

Who thought Andy would name a primadonna
As Rome's Last Hope? It's Mo Johnston. As 'Mojo',
He's a chaser of the flora and the fauna.
He's tanned like a swarthy Byronic hero
(Albeit from the sunbeds at the sauna)
And he's mad and bad and dangerous to oh-know.
    Surely the type of rakish Scottish hero
    Our nation turns its lost and lonely eyes to?

[16] World Cup Willie was the amusingly named mascot of the 1966 World Cup, held in England, and an image of a more innocent age. Ramsey is Sir Alf Ramsey, England World Cup-winning manager and still in charge when Scotland effectively won the World Cup themselves by beating the holders 3-2 at Wembley in 1967.

But he doesn't score. His major contribution
Is sneaking out just post- the post-match parley.
In spite of an explicit prohibition,
Base instinct drives Mo to the grape and barley.
For 'aqua vitae' read 'liquid nutrition',
And he and Bett make headlines: CHAMPAGNE CHARLIES.[17]
    The curfew tolls the knell. In other words,
    In Mojo-speak, it's time to chase the burds.
    The moral, Andy, comes straight from Oor Wullie -
    Ye canna win. They'll just make you look silly.

[17] Not to be confused with the original Champagne Charlie: Charlie Nicholas, of Celtic and Scotland, and later of Sky TV. Charlie left for Arsenal in 1983 (the Rangers fans sang 'Where's Your Charlie Gone?' to the tune of Middle of the Road's 'Chirpy Chirpy Cheep Cheep') and was one of a long line of Scots who found the temptations of London life too difficult to manage. Like Marinello and Cropley before him, his time at Arsenal proved to be a failure relative to his early promise.

4

Now please forgive a crude generalization
(Since plenty Scots are Muslims, Hindus, Sikhs)
And assume for the sake of this narration
That, sure as Donald couldny find his breeks,
Pale colouring's a trademark of our nation,
And our complexion's like our weather – dreich -
        And that safe to say, without being overhasty,
        Our skin tone tends to tend toward the pasty.

Thus good looks for good Scotsmen can prove slippy.
While Spaniards, say, are high-toned, tanned and swarthy,
We're ginger, plukey, pale as Mr Whippy.
Faced with these foreigners more fancy-worthy -
Your slicked-back Latin types - we can be lippy,
And decline to bow and scrape, or curtsey.
        It's a joke as old as time, or even older –
        We Scots are balanced. One chip on each shoulder.

Well, next after that Costa Rica rupture
Comes a challenge in the handsome shape of Sweden.
They're good looking men who have a culture
Forward-looking and reflective of good breeding[18].
Compare their blond hair and their good bone structure
With the results of our inherited poor feeding.
        In the yellow corner, Team Adonis.
        In the blue corner, Team Peely-Wally-Wanness.

---

[18] Having apologised for the racial oversimplification of the Scottish population, I ought to do the same for Sweden. In 2020 '25.9% of the inhabitants of Sweden were from a 'foreign background': that is, each such person either had been born abroad or had been born in Sweden to two parents who themselves had both been born abroad.'

Let me flash you back to 1967,
To a prior match-up of pale white and dark tan,
When the Lisbon Lions[19], a famed Celtic eleven,
Faced a richly handsome *squadra*, Inter Milan's.
How did a team of Jims, Billys and Kevins
Triumph against those fanciest of ran-dans?
    'A game won in the tunnel' - a right old ding-dong,
    Begun when Bertie Auld started a sing-song.[20]

Now national teams come in all shapes and sizes.
Spain make triangles, like it's origami,
While the Germans press 'til the defence capsizes.
The Scottish way's to see it as a rammy
In which the biggest bampot takes the prizes,
And softies greet or call out for their mammy.
    In Genoa we're on this frenzied footing -
    Bertie Auld-like, danders up, the bagpipes tooting.

---

19 The Celtic European Cup-winning team of 1967 was a curiosity as all its members were from the West of Scotland and a far cry from the rainbow nation of more recent Celtic squads. Bobby Lennox was the most exotic, hailing as he did from the tropical climes of Saltcoats, 30 miles down the Ayrshire coast. My old English teacher loved to tell his story of how he was in the Parkhead stands one Saturday and made some 'pointed' remarks about Bobby Lennox. A woman sitting in front turned round and said, with an icy coldness he never forgot, 'I think I should tell you that I'm Mrs Lennox.'

20 At Bertie Auld's funeral, his fellow Lisbon Lion Jim Craig told the story for the thousandth time. As the teams came down the tunnel, the Celtic players, blotchy from a couple of days in the Portuguese sun, lined up alongside an Inter team tanned to a man, clad in cashmere strips, with boots gleaming. 'I suspect, like me, everyone was a bit on the apprehensive side. I have always thought Bertie noticed this and he immediately raised his voice and launched into 'The Celtic Song'. After a minute or two, we all joined in and it certainly helped us to cope with the big occasion.'

'A game won in the tunnel': Us v. Sweden.
As the teams line up, we're growling at them, calling
Out like animals that need their feeding.
McLeish and Aitken, grimacing and bawling,
Big Dave McPherson bringing on eye-bleeding,
Fleck and Leighton toothless - it's appalling...
We're winning ugly[21]! For the Swedes, a shake-up -
To see Braveheart faces, without the blue make-up.

Right from kick-off we're swarming all over them.
McCall (pale, ginger) scores first with a neat flick[22].
The Svelte Svedes can hear a bell toll over them
When Mojo (ginger, freckled) scores a spot-kick.
It's a walk in the park, a pure stroll over them,
And the Tartan Army, belligerent, anarchic,
Can be heard along that Riviera
Putting new words to *Guantanamera*[23].

---

[21] It may be that Scotland had inadvertently trained for such an encounter. Obituaries for Craig Brown, the Scotland manager from 1993-2001, described how teams at squad training matches were sometimes made up of uglies against the rest. Team selection was a matter of considerable controversy. Another way Brown would divvy up the squad for short-sided games, it seems, was to pitch those in the squad who had lost their driving licences versus those who hadn't.

[22] I may have made Stuart McCall's goal sound better than it was. McCall himself is not inclined to be hyperbolic. He described himself as 'deadly from six inches'.

[23] 'We always do it the hard way' was the song overheard on this occasion, to the tune of 'You couldn't score in a brothel'. Although the singing tended to be lusty in the heyday of Scotland's World Cup participation, it was not hugely inventive. The unsuccessful qualifying campaigns since seem to have made the Tartan Army funnier. The various accounts of the fans' travellers' tales delight in incidents such as the famous visit to Torshavn, when they sang 'Save the whale, save the whale/ We're the Famous Tartan Army and we're here to save the whale...' On one of the many recent visits to Jerusalem they stood in front of one of the most sacred sites of the Hebraic world and sang: 'We are wailing/ we are wailing.' All in good taste, of course. The Riviera in question is the Ligurian one, incidentally.

Let wee men tilt at windmills and they'll stand tall.
Is that the lesson of such stirring victories?
Strange that with our backs against a brick wall
And firing squad in front, our valedictory's
To play like champs. Without that curtain-ish call
We play like chumps. Turnips[24]. It's contradictory.
    One take-home from this whole Italia '90
    Is: we sure can turn it on when we've a mind tae.
    Just when you think it's oh, *Sic Transit Gloria,*
    Scotia supplies a wee dose of euphoria.

[24] There is a not very concealed allusion in the final stanza to a 'Sun' headline which followed England's loss to Sweden in the 1990s. The newspaper superimposed a turnip onto the England manager Graham Taylor's head. The report was entitled 'Swedes 2, Turnips 1'.

5

So, help ma boab. (That's Scots, for Jeepers Creepers.)
One theme I haven't touched on is custodians.
(In quaint old football-speak that means goalkeepers.)
How Saint and Greavesie[25] (one for the historians)
Loved to mock our Scottish 'Salmon-Leapers'.
They'd laugh like it was showtime at the Odeon
    At our weakness in the Number One position,
    Their talking heads chortling unto perdition.

[25] 'Saint and Greavesie' was an ITV Saturday lunchtime football show, a low-grade counterpoint to the BBC's Football Focus, which ran from 1985-1992 as a weekly reminder of why my father did not let us watch ITV when we were small. Ian St John (ex-Liverpool and Scotland) and Jimmy Greaves (ex-Tottenham and England) were the hosts, and the programme was constructed almost entirely of feeble banter. Jokes about Scottish goalkeeping (Greaves charmingly liked to refer to 'Jocks') were a familiar trope. In one particularly cringeworthy sequence Greaves watches highlights of a dazzling display in a European tie by Hamish McAlpine of Dundee United. As St John, playing the straight man, shows the saves (which include one from a penalty by Gordon Strachan), Greaves says witless things like 'it deflected and hit him while he was rooted to the spot,' 'the ball hit him while he was holding his hands up in despair,' and 'he was diving out of the way of the penalty and the ball hit him.' McAlpine is then interviewed on the show and Jimmy signs off by saying 'Keep it up, Haggis. I mean Hamish.'

It's true our balls were not always in safe hands.
Frank Haffey[26] was a decent nightclub singer,
But let in nine at Wembley. Live on 'Grandstand',
I saw Kennedy[27] play like a pub ringer -
He hit his own post, then mimicked a hat-stand
As five England goals went in. But chiefly fingered
　　As the target of Ian St John's Epistles
　　Was Alan Rough[28], who played for Partick Thistle.

Permed and pot-bellied, baby-faced yet lanky,
Roughie was lifetime-wedded to calamity.
In my dreams, he gapes like Jimmy Krankie
As Eder chips him. That dream was reality –
The best we had. But now, no more white hankies!
Leighton, Goram, Gunn... A new normality.
　　In answer to our prayers – maybe our cusses -
　　'Keepers have come in threes, like London buses[29].

---

26 Frank Haffey kept goal in 1961 when England beat Scotland 9-3. He was heard singing loudly in the bath afterwards, and later made a living as a cabaret artiste in Australia. Denis Law recalled meeting him there several years after the match; Haffey asked him if it was safe to come out yet. Denis Connaghan, of Celtic, once told me that Jock Stein upbraided him after a poor performance by saying: 'You're as bad as Haffey. In fact, you're worse than Haffey - at least Frank Haffey could sing.'

27 Stewart Kennedy of Rangers conceded five goals to England at Wembley in 1975.

28 Alan Rough was made to look foolish at Espana '82 by Zico and then by Eder, who chipped him while Rough stood gaping like the proverbial pound of mince. Which is what, the Daily Record claimed, he was arrested for pilfering from an Ayr supermarket in 1990.

29 I've not mentioned in this panoply of goalkeeping greatness the Aberdeen goalkeeper Fred Martin, who *twice* let in seven goals while between the Scotland sticks – against Uruguay at the 1954 World Cup, as mentioned, and then, more importantly, against England the following season. Bob Crampsey, a doyen of Scottish football writers (and the husband of one of my mother's best friends) said that Martin 'looked like an inside forward who had gone into goal as a stop-gap.'

So all's well as we reach the Alpi stadium,
Where Brazilians are being mobbed by dancing cuties.
Their bodies, trimmed and waxed in the gymnasium,
Are models of first-rate aesthetic beauty.
Near the buses parked by this football palladium
The Tartan Army shake more hirsute booties,
        And play their due role in the scenic saga
        By offering the Brazilians Tennent's Lager.

This Brazil team's not their greatest iteration
But still has names (Romario, Careca)
That bathe my brow in fulsome perspiration.
Dunga *et al* can drive a double decker
Through any thoughts of our qualification.
By custom they're our regular hope-wrecker.
        Our best hope is that they might leave some stars out,
        For they've qualified, and could have the cigars out.

It looks that way when it kicks off – vanilla -
But I'm praying that our team don't get too lary,
For these samba boys are not unlike gorillas -
You make them angry, they get proper scary.
Who could forget, in Spain, in old Sevilla?
We took the lead with that 'toe-poke' from Narey[30].
        No-one sane thought it would be a shoo-in,
        But we didn't just get beat. We got a doing.

---

[30] David Narey, of Dundee United, scored the opening goal when Scotland played Brazil in Seville in 1982. He collected a knockdown from John Wark, stepped forward and smashed the ball into the top corner. Jimmy Hill, the underslung BBC commentator, who was never a figure of admiration in Scotland in the first place (at school in the 1970s we would banterously suggest someone was talking rubbish by stroking our chins in imitation of Hill's goatee) secured his place in Scottish football demonology by describing the shot, in his half-time summary, as a 'toe-poke'. Revenge, of course, is a dish best served warm and washed down with a few pints of McEwan's. Generations of Scotland fans have sung his name in a chant too 'nuanced' to quote in full here.

This time we're lower-key - but qualifying.
'Narey' a shot on goal. Nil-nil at half time!
Then Aitken nearly scores. It's mortifying -
Fate-and-Jimmy-Greaves-having-a-laugh time -
For the Kraken wakes. There's some token defying,
'Til Jim lets one slip like it's the soap at bathtime,
        And Muller pops it in. Hugh McIlvanney[31]
        (To summarise) said Leighton was a fanny.

Then with seconds left, and Scotland on the way out,
The ball breaks out to Mojo. There's no man on.
Maurice strikes it sweetly from six yards out.
That ball moves like it's been shot from a cannon,
But Taffarel, their goalie, throws his hand out,
And leaps, as Greaves would say, like a 'scotch' salmon.
        That Brazilian goalies normally were chronic
        Adds a twist that some might call ironic.
        Had it gone in it would have been a screamer,
        Worth its own canto of *ottava rima*.

---

31 Hugh McIlvanney rhymes with fanny. If you can have more than one doyen at the same time, McIlvanney was the doyen of Scottish football writers. His portentous style was memorably parodied by Jonathan Watson in the first 'Only An Excuse' broadcast on BBC Radio Scotland in 1987. ('The first officially recorded football match in Scotland took place in 1314, immediately after the Battle of Bannockburn, when two teams of Scots kicked the severed head of an Englishman to and fro across the bloody battlefield. It was a poor game, with defences well on top, and few genuine goalmouth incidents…') What McIlvanney actually wrote in response to Leighton's mistake in this match was that Scotland's exit 'owed much to a blunder by their goalkeeper that was in keeping with a suicidal tradition.'

6

So that is that. Again, we're no princesses.
We've found another way to get nowhere.
As per, our Cinderellas in blue dresses
Are home before the prince brings the footwear.
No massive highs or lows, no great excesses,
Just a couple sent out to the naughty stair.
        As a replay of old flaws it's been uncanny -
        But if Scotland had no baws she'd be your granny.

Now different nations have their melancholies.
In Galicia they talk about *saudade* –
Sadness for those who've left in search of lolly.
There's the loneliness of the long-distance Paddy,
While Turks are sad owing to their past folly -
They've lost the empire built by their grandaddies[32].
        We've our own take on what the Turks call *hüzün* -
        Sadness that comes from coming home just too-zoon.

---

[32] These are very specific melancholies, unlike the more generalised *ennui, angst* or *toksa. Saudade* is vividly described in the novels of the Galician novelist Manuel Rivas. Galicians for many years used the sea as an escape from poverty and from the Civil War; there is a very significant Galician exile population in Argentina, for example. The equally brilliant Nobel laureate Orhan Pamuk, in his book 'Istanbul: Memories and the City', ascribes the city's residents' liking for black clothes to *hüzün*, which he claims is an abiding sense of loss arising from the end of the Ottoman Empire.

But what happened next? Well Andy, evangelical,
Kept trying to change our habits for the better.
It turned out that it was a cause chimerical,
As we in self-destruction stayed enfettered.
But he stayed on at the helm – calm, unhysterical -
Ignoring all the fuds and the bedwetters
 Whose succulent lamb-eating[33] tittle-tattle
 Suggested he lacked readiness for battle.

Jim Leighton? The big scene in his bi-opic
Would show Sir Alex Ferguson being callous,
And poor Jim (half-blind, mind, mole-like, and myopic)
Getting hair-dried for that match with Crystal Palace.
Jim came back up the road and, periscopic,
Resurfaced beneath the Aurora Borealis.
 He's a great man, who rose above the haver -
 Though he really should have gone down to Specsavers[34].

---

[33] 'Succulent lamb eating' is a term of disdain for a sycophantic strain in Scottish football journalism, particularly in relation to uncritical reporting of Rangers during the chairmanship of Sir David Murray in the 1990s. 'Fans with typewriters' is one thing; the issue becomes more complex when they are Old Firm fans with typewriters. The journalist Graham Speirs defined it thus: 'Succulent lamb journalism means a culture... of sycophantic, unquestioning, puff journalism that went on around Rangers generally and Sir David Murray particularly.'

[34] After his disastrous FA Cup semi-final showing, for which he was pilloried, Jim Leighton successfully rebuilt his career with Hibs and Aberdeen, and played at a third World Cup in 1998. If the reference to Specsavers seems wanton, it's not; in the 1986 World Cup qualifier versus Wales at Ninian Park, he lost a contact lens late in the first half and had no replacement. The veteran Alan Rough was on the bench and at half time was warming up with David Speedie of Chelsea, playing a silly game in which they were trying to knock the helmets off the Welsh Guards' bandsmen with the ball. The physio emerged from the changing-room to tell Rough he had to go in and get warmed up; Rough, thinking it was a wind-up, didn't. As he came back up the tunnel he met Jock Stein, livid because Rough had not come as demanded. Stein greeted him as follows: 'You're on, Rough, you fat bastard'. Stein died of a heart attack towards the end of that match, in which a 1-1 draw all but secured Scotland's place in Mexico. The much-maligned Rough kept a clean sheet in the half he played, but was apparently upset that these had been Stein's last words to him.

And Mojo! Don Juan reborn! You can't elude us,
For you're the man who, dauntless, faced down danger,
Signing first for Celtic then, like Brutus,
Betraying Caesar for the Glasgow Rangers[35].
The Celtic fans still like to call you Judas.
The Rangers fans called you 'dog in the manger'.
    It's a rare day when the Glasgow bigot voice speaks
    A single thought from out both of its bum-cheeks.

But I'll sign off with one final tale of slapstick.
In that last game there's handbags, argy-barging.
Once it's clear that Branco's lining up the free kick,
That the defensive wall will need enlarging
Does not require knowledge encyclopaedic.
MacLeod says he'll attack the ball, come charging.
    The rest, cupping their teacakes, give their backing,
    But it's a tiger's smile. The ball does the attacking.

---

[35] In point of fact Mojo had already joined Rangers before the 1990 tournament. He had by all accounts agreed to sign for Celtic from Nantes, then changed his mind, for reasons no doubt partly financial given the Celtic board's celebrated 'biscuit tin' approach to transfers. Celtic fans registered an official WE HATE MO JOHNSTON branch of the Celtic Supporters' Club. Rangers fans meanwhile burned their season tickets and laid wreaths at Ibrox Park to mark what was seen as the end of the great tradition of the club refusing to sign Catholics. All of which was a bit futile, since it later emerged that Catholic players had been surreptitiously playing in the team well before the influx of Sign-of-the-Cross wielding Italians signed by Graeme Souness. For example, Don Kichenbrand, a South African Catholic, had signed for Rangers in 1955 and played many games for them; he even joined an Orange Lodge by way of disguise.

Branco's left foot apes a nuclear fusion.
This shot heard round the world makes a percussion
That bounces Murdo's bonce into confusion.
As Elvis sang, it's only fools that rush in -
He almost scores, but under the illusion
That our goal is Brazil's. It's the concussion -
    On the greatest night of a decent career, his
    Brain can't tell where New York or New Year is.

Although his cerebellum's somersaulting
Murdo spurns the magic sponge, naysaying
When the trainer tries to get the smelling salts in.
He doesn't know which way his team is playing!
And this is Scotland - getting a last waltz in,
But still not really sure quite what we're daein.
    Now were it not that fat-shaming is wrongful,
    It'd be time to give the large lady her songful -
    While it just would not be right to sing Puccini
    In an itsy-bitsy polka-dot bikini.
    So let's leave Italia with Paul Gascoigne tearful[36] -
    Crying for Scotland, and our missing years-ful.

---

[36] Gazza is the not usually lachrymose Paul Gascoigne, of England. As immortalised in the Walker's Crisps adverts of the period, he cried when booked in England's semi-final, when he realised the caution would keep him out of the final had England made it. (Which they didn't, in which fact I take no pleasure whatsoever; they were knocked out on penalties by West Germany, playing their last World Cup before Reunification.) Gascoigne ended up joining Rangers in 1995, famously and foolishly adopting some on-pitch orange-flute-playing-to-the-gallery gestures. He also played a significant role in knocking Scotland out of the European championships in 1996. As for the missing years: to much wailing and gnashing of teeth, Scotland failed to qualify for the finals held in the USA in 1994.

1998

Eddie Gray's Elegy

For PGW (1923-2013)

Though they lament the end of things, elegies offer a hint of injury-time consolation. As every schoolchild knows, the British are not as adept at the technical side of the poetry game as the continentals. Since elegiac couplets in the classical style require fancy footwork difficult to achieve in English, poets like Thomas Gray (no relation to Eddie, Frank or Andy) developed the no-nonsense Route One elegiac stanza used here.

France, 1998

World Cup Group A

10 June 1998, 4.30 pm

Brazil	**2**	**Scotland**	**1**
Sampaio 5, Boyd (og) 74		Collins 38 (pen)	
Stade de France, Saint-Denis			80,000

16 June 1998, 4.30 pm

Scotland	**1**	**Norway**	**1**
Burley 66		Flo 46	
Parc Lescure, Bordeaux			31,800

23 June 1998, 8.00 pm

Scotland	**0**	**Morocco**	**3**
		Bassir 23 85, Hadda 46	
Stade Geoffroy Guichard, Saint-Etienne			30,600

Group C Table	W	D	L	F	A	Pts
Brazil (Q)	2	0	1	6	3	6
Norway (Q)	1	2	0	5	4	5
Morocco	1	1	1	5	5	4
Scotland	0	1	2	2	6	1

Scotland did not qualify for the second stage.

'It was a perfect Summer, as all World Cup summers are...'
(Karl Ove Knausgaard, *Home and Away*)

I

The curfew tolls the knell of parting day
When the news at six pops up on the TV
Or the 'Reporting Scotland' theme-tune plays
And you plod in from the study for your tea.

You're seventy-five. A wonder, in a way -
Working at home is no Professors' Square,
But you're still at the books the live-long day.
Slower, but, as we all say, still all there,

Still all day in that study. It's strange to find
The way we were still holds when I come back.
You out of our sight, we out your mind.
The shut door dulls the typewriter's sharp clack.

I'm here to clear the attic of some weight.
Just things. Not the air. Not things unsaid.
Just things, in boxes, of uncertain date,
That bend the boards above your aged head.

We shall not be moved. Maybe I will -
By these school reports, the college magazines.
By this photograph, of my face and a girl's,
Cheek-to-apple-cheek in that machine,

That curtained booth at Central. Now her name
Escapes me - as did she - though I've kept by
This programme for the Czechoslovakia game -
Another night when true love made me cry.

The Subbuteo comes down - Brazil, Peru.
The Scalextric cars. The decalled Airfix planes.
And then some things that coin a link to you -
The treasures of our days, the lost remains

Of smoky, threadbare years of low supply.
When petrol empires feared decline and fall
They lured their hard-up customers to buy
With giveaways, and we'd collect them all,

As if free stuff was a way we could recoup
The 'cost of living' - the time and money spent.
Tumblers, cups and mugs. Bowls for our soup,
To warm us through winters of discontent.

We'd commemorative coins, like 'Man In Flight' -
They offset for a while the plunging pound.
'Great Britons' – back then, History was white.
'Historical Cars' - for what went round, came round,

Rotating with the seasons. But the best
Of the collect-and-keeps were football-themed.
Four gallons for a sticker of a crest,
Say, to post on to your fold-out chart of teams.

And here they are. Footballers deified
On coins struck for Mexico in tarnished tin.
For us, false coins, since we'd not qualified,
And English monarchs never were our kings,

But Jinky and Gemmell sit amongst the gods
Resinned in these busts from Cleveland Fuels.
'71 - 'Joe Mercer's Britain Squad' -
Our days of wine and roses. Football pools.

And here are the Esso badges from that year,
That season, still stuck to the card beneath.
By now they'd made sure that our teams were there.
Seeing Dundee, Falkirk and Cowdenbeath

Carries me back there with a tender shock.
Getting petrol got me out the door
For my fuel crisis - watching that pump clock
Clank tiredly round, mechanically, to four -

For if it made it, you'd come from the booth
With the prize, a packet tossed through to the back.
Throwaway riches. Penny for the youth.
(I say riches. There was a 'starter pack'

Of twenty, maybe, other dads might buy -
But you weren't that way inclined, and don't forget
That pester-power was just pie in the sky,
Was like back seat-belts - not invented yet.)

We knew enough to say our grace and smile,
Grateful for what we got, even just one.
It could be Charlton, for the swapping pile,
Or the grail no one had seen, Huddersfield Town.

Though I know these unearthed shards of our shared days
Are midden-scraps of archaeology,
And there for next to nothing on eBay,
I knock the study door – 'A cup of tea?' -

And show you. You say, as you always say,
'Terrific,' but your side-eyed smile is thin.
Giving it time, but not the time of day.
Your mind's elsewhere, perhaps on Latin hymns,

And for a second we are gauchely paired -
Me standing by, you sitting at your desk.
I shut the door, go back to climbing stairs,
Go back to clearing out. The present task.

2

Thinking back, might we have watched this one –
France '98, I mean - just you and I,
Together? When the clearing out was done
And I scrambled down my ladder from the sky,

Did you come down from your ivory tower? If so,
It's a collector's piece, a lost treasure.
In '70 I see you, clear as day
Watching Coleman's roundups of the day before,

But '74 is grandad's, and by '78
I'm in the pub with pals and sliding down
That chute you never climb back up. That gate,
That door, shuts fast. What's done can't be undone.

Empires have fallen while we've been away.
Sic transit gloria mundi. Just eight years,
But the Yugoslavs, those Czechs, East Germany
Have vanished from the map since we were here.

Rules, like frontiers, change. You can't pass back,
Waste time. The football's gone 'dilute to taste' -
Gone are the days you'd not go in the book
Even if you cut your man off at the waist.

But we've scrubbed up well – we're now dressed to succeed.
Gone are the cheap and shiny Burton suits.
Our squad is sporting kilts and Harris tweed,
While the Tartan Army's keen-eyed new recruits

Aren't the ragtag mob of yesteryear.
That feather-cut home-made-flagged mob of clowns
Who, pissed on Tennent's Super, liked to tear
Up the town or pull the goalposts down

Now keep themselves in line, and they profess
Only good cheer as they dispense their pearls
Of wit and wisdom. They should have a crest:
'Purveyors of Good Humour to the World'.

Their chant is that they're here to save the snail.
Their chat is this time luck must go our way.
For if Empires fall, so can the epic fail -
Motif of all our World Cup yesterdays.

Eyes of the world. We have the opening game.
The future's ginger at the Stade de France
And the See-You-Jimmys call us by our name.
When Brazil come out the tunnel holding hands,

Craig Brown tells our team they've shat their breeks
At the mere sight of our boys, our lion-hearts
Who in the anthem-lines puff out their cheeks.
All's going so well. But then the football starts.

Another chant goes up – 'what will, will be' –
That's sad but true. With just five minutes gone
We're one behind. A Collins penalty
Means we're not trailing them for very long,

And the second half is tense, a grown-up test.
Late on, it's chipped to Cafù, on their wing.
He pulls it back. It hits Jim on the chest,
There's body-part ping-pong, it bounces in –

So much for Lady Luck's bosom embrace.
But there's no time to brood. On to Bordeaux.
Losing to Brazil is no disgrace,
We say. Move on. It's Norway next. We know

That they're a 'long ball team', in quotes,
So *Vikings, Row the Boat Ashore*'s the chant.
They've helmets, with the horns. Long ball, long boats.
If you're going to rape and pillage, clap your hands –

But the joke's on us. Like luck, the ref is blind.
He gives our stonewaller outside the box.
Dailly heads wide, and then we fall behind
To Havard Flo, some Scandi-blond lummox.

We steal a point when Burley rolls one in,
So we're still in with a shout. Cometh the hour,
Cometh our men down to St-Etienne,
Singing *Only a Pylon!* at the Eiffel Tower.

But oh, Morocco. How we fluff our lines,
For all the song and dance. For all the noise.
Post-imperial, we've missed the signs,
Still thinking African means whipping-boys

When the 'great unwashed', it seems, have the whip hand.
Our noisy neighbours from the *banlieux*
Of Paris, Brussels, Lille and Amsterdam
See Bashir score, and then Hadda breaks through -

Accessing his inner Alan Rough,
Leighton palms his shot into our net.
When Burley, name and nature, gets sent off
For a fly kick at someone's calf, all bets

Are off. A third, Bashir again. The scenes
At the Moroccan end! Outsung, outfought,
We're a bona fide end of empire team.
Declined, fallen, all out of luck. But wait -

See, poor Morocco go out anyway
After Brazil, of all the banker teams,
Lose to the Route One Vikings of Norway.
Had we won, so would we. It maybe means

We *were* lucky. We dodged that twist of Fate.
A swan sings: *We're shite, but we drink champagne.*
But it's not so much a party as a wake,
For we're home before the postcards yet again.

3

Now I said we watched together. But did we?
You were never one for that louche line
Of crumpled cans, or dinner on your knee.
You shunned the drivel dished out at half time,

The platitudes after the whistle blew.
Warm in the halo of your reading lamp
You'd better things to do than listen to
Hazel Irvine live from Scotland's camp.

While I'd have been in place right from the start,
You'd have drifted in and out the den.
A quick check of the score, then you'd depart.
Ghosting in: now there, now gone again.

That's how it was, how it would always be
With you. Days were for work. A kind of crime
To let one slip. Day-shifts at the Uni,
Then work when you came home. No wasting time,

For that was middle class. You thanked your stars
Your hard-knock life had freed you from white noise.
Let weaker wills play golf, drink wine, keep cars -
Or watch whole World Cup matches with their boys.

You weren't forbidding. No, you'd drink a gin,
Or sit down with the crossword after tea,
And in the kitchen, wiping round, you'd sing
Old dance-hall numbers ('I know she likes me

Because she says so') as you'd wash and rinse.
You'd brainiacal party tricks you'd play.
Converting guineas into pounds and pence -
'Ready Reckoning' – or reciting Gray.

But graft is what boot-strapped you, fair is fair -
From a two-room, nine-kid, outside-privy home
To a different sort of throne, an ancient chair
In the language of declining, falling Rome.

Your brains being in your head and not your feet
Football was mine alone. I'd climb the wall
To play, up in the park by Arthur's Seat,
Italian boys staying at the Pollok Halls.

When picked for Holy Cross from time to time
(It was the janny's job, back then, to name the team)
I wouldn't look for your face on the line.
You didn't do the sidelined father scene.

You let me go to games. You didn't go,
Of course, but from seven or eight
Would slip me two-and-six for Easter Road.
I'd trouser it, get lifted at the gate

By someone else's dad, and there, with friends,
I learned the stranger's tongue. The songs we sang
About razors and chains as we changed ends
Were a far, far cry from your arms and the man.

Just once or twice you'd yield. '72.
The League Cup Final. Celtic. Pester-powered,
For once, you came to Hampden, took me through
To save me from the neds. When Stanton scored

You tried to help a boy with a slashed head.
Eggheaded, in your raincoat and your specs,
You offered him your hanky then, instead,
Rebuffed, backed off, retreated to that desk.

So I didn't think you liked it. But you did.
It came as a surprise - a Hampden, 'at home' truth -
When you said you'd been before, to see Madrid,
With Puskas in his pomp, you in your youth,

While your brother told me when he came around
That as a boy you'd 'Uruguayan' moves
In back-alley games behind two up, two downs.
One pair of boots between the two of you,

The legend went, so you played in the side.
Younger, but better. He showed me a snap,
A team photo. You're wiry, shadow-eyed.
Those boots. A ghostly white shirt. A tank top.

I wonder why it was you didn't say?
Why you didn't kick a garden ball around?
Show off those moves, or spend your Saturdays
On some red blaes, some muddy common ground?

For, now and then, there was a verbal tic
That showed that shadowed eye, that secret self.
You'd come in, ask the score. Then pause, or stick
Around, momently, back to the bookshelf,

And watch the action with an eagle eye
I've never had. You would rarely enthuse.
Instead you'd issue these impatient sighs
And heirloom phrases I wish I could use.

Suppose some trier – say, Tosh McKinlay -
Couldn't see a pass and lost the ball.
Oh, send him a postcard, I would hear you say,
As if there'd been a time before this all

When this was all there was and you - you too -
Had a terrace voice. Hearing that sound
In my head now, I'd share my bob with you -
Let someone's dad lift us into the ground.

I stand outside your study, in the hall.
It's a kickaround, three and in, with your ghost.
A cold day. Rub and blow. It's goalie's ball.
Words pass back and forth. Breath, warm as toast.

4

Well, Craig Brown says he wouldn't change a thing.
'We don't have a Ronaldo, a Zidane.'
Silk purse, sow's ear. A Jack can't be a King.
'At this time we don't breed that sort of man.'

That is his postmortem: 'can but try',
But, future-wise, we're doomed. He sees our state,
Does Craig. Doing well just to qualify.
Historically, the ball is on the slates -

Decline and fall. Soon we'll be Israel.
Moldova. Malta. Minnows, off the pace.
North Macedonia. 'And just as well
That we don't have to play the whole damn place.'

You always liked that kind of joke, of course.
The suppository. 'For all the good it did
I might as well have shoved it up my arse' –
Maybe laughing at that was when you slid

Off the kerb and fell down in the road.
In Scarborough it was. We thought the sun
Had blinded you, but we were blind. It showed
A premortem, foreshadowed what would come.

First fall, and then decline. The wrong way round.
Some Parkinsonsish weakness in the brain
That shook its spider movement through your hand.
You won't see Scotland at a Cup again,

In the fifteen years you've left - a small mercy
Masking the hard truth that you'll not see through
Your plans and projects for posterity.
You tried to not waste time. Time wasted you.

As in that study less and less gets done,
We keep a watching brief and fail to act.
We join you in your silence, keeping mum.
We make a waste land and we call it tact -

A feeble excuse for our idle tongues,
For the silent treatment, rubbing like a sore
From man to man, from fathers to their sons,
This 'watching what we say'. But something more –

My brother says in your last months and days,
He'd find you, slow-escaping, in the hall.
Hunched over the radio, he says,
Finding a way to listen to football,

To David Begg, maybe, in commentary,
Counting down the minutes at Parkhead.
You'd look absorbed, as if finally free,
The voice outside the one inside your head.

That attic trove I found – its well-thumbed shine -
Reminds me that the more recent the Cup
The more the detail fades. Who won last time?
Short-term. It's gone. I'd have to look it up.

But '74? I can kick every ball.
I don't mean only two points for a win
Or old man stuff about the pass-back rule.
I'll tell you how Brazil's third goal went in

Against Zaire, describe the Haiti team,
How Holland had dirty Brazil on toast,
Poland's midfield, the Two Germanies game -
Not just how Bremner put it past the post.

Back then is when I best remember you.
When we did see a match, you'd do this thing.
If, coming home by bus, there was a queue,
You'd eye the baleful, smoky post-match line

And, saying we should try at the next stop,
Set out on foot into the falling gloam.
The tenements would light above, the shops
Darken below. A forced march towards home.

Buses would pass, lit windows wet with breath.
You'd eye the crowds inside, pronounce them packed
And keep walking, though we were sick to death,
And far too big to carry on your back.

You led the way. Of course, you'd not say much,
As if by being there you'd done your share -
While we, victims of Zeno's paradox,
Felt always halfway home, never quite there.

We shall not be moved. It's been decades
Since France, when Scotland laboured at the Cup,
And I laboured on the boards above your head.
In such missing years you might look up,

Say you don't know what you've got until it's gone.
A blessed time? It was, for all the pain,
And prompts the question we hear in the song -
Just when will we see your like again?

I asked that when I bore you, shoulder high,
Carrying you like a hero from the field.
So close, and yet so far. My eyes still dry,
I fell in step. 'Ach, just follow the crowd,'

The undertaker smiled. Mud caked my boots
In divots. Headstones, with their names and dates,
Terraced the hill. Men stripped in their dark suits
Criss-crossed the hole with boards to take the weight,

And as they lowered you, I strained to see -
To peer into the space, behold the man.
You've left this world to darkness and to me.
Send me a postcard, father, if you can.

Also by STEPHEN WALSH

Prose

HEARTACHE SPOKEN HERE (Viking/ Penguin)

'Country & Western's *Fever Pitch*' (Independent on Sunday)

'An unusual & highly original book, full of warmth, humour, insight & optimism' (Terence Blacker, Sunday Times)

'By far the best, & one of the most underrated travel books of the year' (Sarah Wheeler, Daily Telegraph Books of the Year)

FAITHFUL DEPARTURES (Viking/Penguin)

'When approaching a pilgrimage, put your faith in Stephen Walsh' (Hugh MacDonald, The Herald)

'Delightful… populated by extraordinary characters and events… insightful, humorous and full of humanity' (Sunday Express)

'An immaculate concept' (Independent)

VOICES OF THE OLD FIRM (Mainstream)

'Full of great yarns and fascinating football stories. An excellent read for students not only of the beautiful game, but of Scottish culture, urban conflict and macaroon bars' (Steve McGookin, Financial Times)

'Highly entertaining' (Roddy Forsyth, FourFourTwo)

'A book that has become something of a classic in the social history of football' (Daily Telegraph)

Poetry

AN ELECTORATE OF TURKEYS - *The Twelve Villanelles of Christmas* (CHapbooks)

'Lively, witty and formally dazzling. What more can a reader want from poems about Christmas?' (Daljit Nagra)

WALKING IN THE RUINS - *Translations from N S Sigogo* (CHapbooks)

'Memorable, strong, living poetry that gives root to experience, story and 'forestfuls' of songs…' (Sasha Dugdale)